TSUNAMI

by Joyce Markovics

Consultant:
Paul Whitmore, Director
National Oceanic and Atmospheric Administration's
National Tsunami Warning Center

BEARPORT
PUBLISHING

New York, New York

23.93
4/14 BaT

Credits

Cover, © AFLO/MAINICHI NEWSPAPER/EPA/Newscom; 4–5, © Stefan Ernst; 6–7, © AFP/Getty Images; 8–9, © Downunderphotos; 10–11, © littlesam/Shutterstock; 12–13, © Tatiana Morozova/Alamy; 14–15, © Getty Images; 16–17, © Karin Hildebrand Lau/Shutterstock; 18–19, © AFP/Getty Images; 20–21, © STR/epa/Corbis; 22, © Georgios Alexandris/Shutterstock; 23TL, © Prometheus72/Shutterstock; 23TR, © Mehmet Cetin/Shutterstock; 23BL, © underwater graphics; 23BR, © AFP/Getty Images.

Publisher: Kenn Goin
Senior Editor: Joyce Tavolacci
Creative Director: Spencer Brinker
Design: Debrah Kaiser
Photo Researcher: We Research Pictures, LLC

Library of Congress Cataloging-in-Publication Data in process at time of publication (2014)
Library of Congress Control Number: 2013034719
ISBN-13: 978-1-62724-130-4

For more information, write to Bearport Publishing Company, Inc., 45 West 21st Street, Suite 3B, New York, New York 10010. Printed in the United States of America.

10 9 8 7 6 5 4 3 2 1

CONTENTS

TSUNAMIS

Swoosh!

A huge wave races
toward a beach.

A **tsunami** is coming!

4

Tsunami is a Japanese word. It means "**harbor** wave."

The giant wave reaches the beach.

Crash!

It spills onto land.

It covers everything with water.

A tsunami can be one wave or a group of waves.

Most waves are caused by wind.

Tsunamis are different.

They are often caused by **earthquakes**.

About 80 percent of tsunamis occur in the Pacific Ocean.

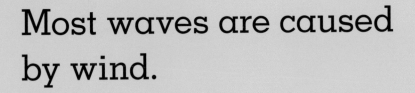

ARCTIC OCEAN
Asia
North America
ATLANTIC OCEAN
PACIFIC OCEAN
INDIAN OCEAN
Australia
South America
SOUTHERN OCEAN
Antarctica
N
W
E
S

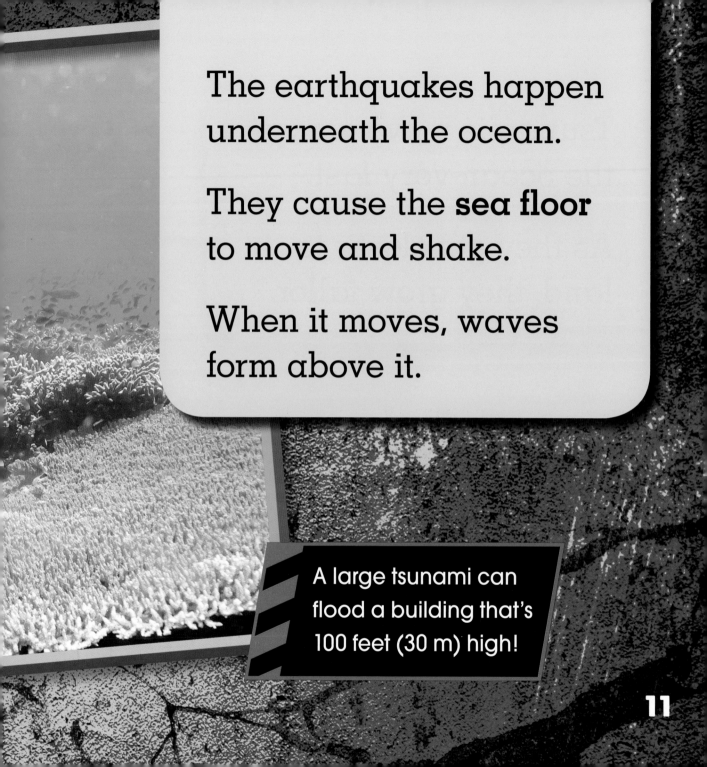

The earthquakes happen underneath the ocean.

They cause the **sea floor** to move and shake.

When it moves, waves form above it.

A large tsunami can flood a building that's 100 feet (30 m) high!

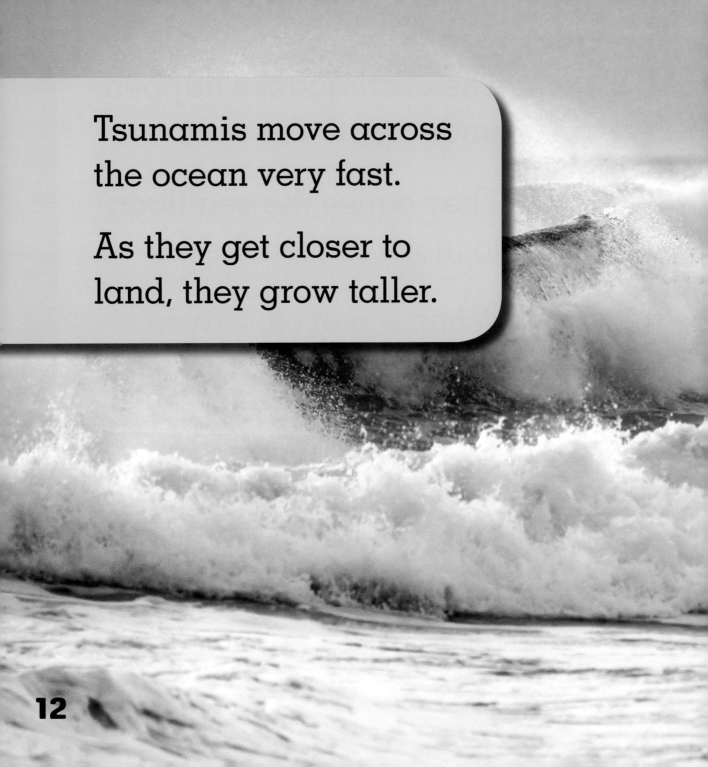

Tsunamis move across the ocean very fast.

As they get closer to land, they grow taller.

Tsunamis can travel up to 600 miles per hour (967 kph). That's about as fast as a jet!

Tsunamis can cause lots of damage.

Their waves can sweep away houses.

They can destroy whole towns.

In 2011, a tsunami in Japan destroyed more than 300,000 buildings.

How can you tell a tsunami is coming?

If you feel an earthquake and you are near the sea, move away.

Listen to the radio or TV for a tsunami warning.

If you see water in the ocean move away from the beach, be careful. A tsunami may be on its way.

To stay safe, move away from the sea.

Go to higher ground.

You may only have minutes to escape.

If you are in a tall building, go to the highest floor. It will be harder for the tsunami to reach you.

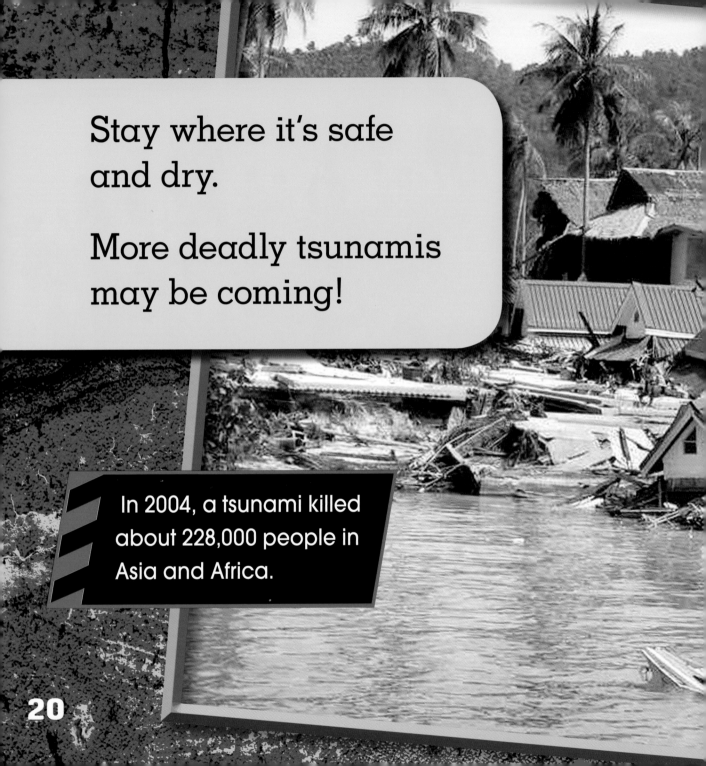

Stay where it's safe and dry.

More deadly tsunamis may be coming!

In 2004, a tsunami killed about 228,000 people in Asia and Africa.

TSUNAMI FACTS

- Tsunamis can travel many miles onto land. They can flood huge areas.

- Hawaii has more tsunamis than any other state in America—about one per year.

- A tsunami that hit Alaska in 1958 was 1,700 feet (518 m) tall. That's taller than the Empire State Building!

GLOSSARY

earthquakes (URTH-*kwayks*) a shaking of the ground caused by the sudden movement of rocks below Earth's surface

harbor (HAR-bur) an area of water near shore where ships can stay or unload goods

sea floor (SEE *flor*) the bottom of the ocean

tsunami (tsoo-NAH-mee) a group of waves usually caused by an underwater earthquake

23

INDEX

READ MORE

Park, Louise. *Tsunamis (Natural Disasters).* North Mankato, MN: Smart Apple Media (2008).

Stiefel, Chana. *Tsunamis (A True Book).* New York: Children's Press (2009).

LEARN MORE ONLINE

To learn more about tsunamis, visit
www.bearportpublishing.com/ItsaDisaster!

ABOUT THE AUTHOR

Joyce Markovics lives along the Hudson River in Tarrytown, New York, far from the reach of terrifying tsunamis.